Chromatic Tales

Stories Painted in Every Hue

Neha Pandey

BookLeaf Publishing

India | USA | UK

Dedication

To the one I wanted to make proud.

Preface

Colors are more than pigments on a canvas; they are emotions, memories, and echoes of untold stories. *Chromatic Tales* is an anthology where each hue breathes life into a narrative. From the defiant glow of magenta rebellion to the deceptive silver of a trickster's tongue, these poems explore the shades of human experience. The golden ambitions of a thief, the maroon fatigue of a laborer, the peach-soft strength of a gentle heart. Every piece is a thread in this woven tapestry of color and meaning.

This collection is not just an artistic exploration of hues but a journey through the depth of emotions they hold. Whether it is the quiet grief of a colorless bride or the neon ecstasy of a bustling city, each poem invites you to see beyond the surface, to feel the pulse of the world painted in every shade.

Let these verses take you through corridors of nostalgia and alleys of rebellion.

Here, colors speak, and stories unfold in their embrace.

Acknowledgements

To all those who share their stories, who paint their worlds with words. Your voices echo in mine.
And to my friend from the island in the seas, who reads between my lines, thank you!

Miss Mary's Blue Veil

Miss Mary's counsel,
Taught all something.
Women and men in awe,
Admired endlessly.
Click and clack down the street,
Her blue umbrella ambled.

Erickson's daughter,
Five and beautiful,
Steamed her ears,
Sobbing behind the stage.
Miss Mary's words, soft and fade,
Calmed the girl's veins.

Hidden eyes,
Smiles so bright,
A troubleshooter in an aqua frock,
Soothed all living-kind.
Jumping kids always asked,
"Miss, how are you so smart?"

Her umbrella grew a shade darker
With every dialogue she played.
Mrs. to Miss, she changed

After the beast she loved faded away.
Lost in blue, this phoenix grew,
Now puffs her pains away

Grey Collar

Tony's shirt was pale and grey,
A tie that never swayed.
A fading shadow of the guy,
Beneath the dull and clouded sky.

He never saw his child play,
But sat in cubicles that preyed.
He longed and craved his Mrs.' tray,
But swallowed the taste of the office buffet.

Hands that once dug the clay,
Now wrote emails across the day.
His soul wandered as a stray,
When he turned to ashes grey.

A Hue That Stays

Samara undid her leathery shoes.
Daintily fixed her dress.
Sipped the chai her mother brewed.
Relaxed in her brown chair.

Gazed at the cabinets, so still.
Stuffed with clutter,
they had no say in.
Motionless, yet bearing it all.

Books tinted in ancient pigment,
Weighed on her wooden shelves.
Sepia Polaroids as little bookmarks
Were keepsakes in themselves.

She followed the dust to the amber pane.
The bark outside, engraved her name.
The hue had seeped into her bubble,
And so she stayed and tore the letter.

Crimson Window

Her windows are crimson tint
Bed covered in satin sheets.
Those who lay beneath the fabric
Called her the charming queen.
These weaklings with power,
weigh down on her with their sin.

The courtesan plays it well.
She smiles, taps, and manipulates,
binds them not with chains, but air,
converts their desires to needs.
A thirst never quenched,
pleased only with her skin bare.

She survived her toil and grief,
Now she gets to choose kings.
Nobody expected the riches
the courtesan had tucked in.
She struggled to breathe,
drowning in unreturned gifts.

And so she quietly left,
fleeing chains of gold.
Some will weep and wail.

Claiming she was theirs.
Little do the nitwits know,
she never belonged to them

Arrest at the Golden Valley

All jaws dropped
and gasped from belly.
There was an arrest
at the Golden Valley.

Lootin' Louis, in metal bands,
Lost his pride
before his friends
and his nasty bride.

Louis started looting
when his mother passed away in cold.
While he cried for rooting,
Soon learned hunger favors bold.

No vault was secure.
No lock he couldn't unbraid.
His name would ensure
The guards remained afraid.

They'd search for clues,
but none would remain.
He'd twist and use
their fragile brain.

He swam in fame
and chose his story.
The thirst for glory,
His ultimate aim.

He had left no precious ore,
nor diamond, ruby, emerald.
After a heist, tired and sore,
His bride's dare was *the ultimate gold.*

The ultimate gold
in the Golden Valley
was for a small hold
before the king's men could tally.

Conned as a protector,
He opened the door.
It shone so bright,
he froze to the core.

In stormed the men
with axes and swords.
Lootin' Louis ran,
Pleading to the Lord.

The shrewd bride lied,

Her tears stayed dried.
His greed for pride,
Led to his demise.

Last Light on the Sea

Little scout was at a cliff,
Watching the orange star sink.
Its ember warmed his heart within,
The autumn glow embraced him.
All his worries tumbled down the hill,
Melted into the waves so free,
At the sight of the orange sea.
Exhausted, his soul
Was now at peace.

The White Canvas

The canvas was white and peeled,
The painter's hand stained her deep.
He traced her edges
And taped her tight,
For every buyer who stripped her bare.

His strokes of greed,
And paint that reeked,
All fell to decay.
After the burglar fled
With the canvas in sway.

Together they colored,
The water, so milk,
A sun that smiled,
Grass that sung,
And flowers that grinned.

She danced in snowfall.
Together with clouds,
She bathed in light.
In the hush of endless bright,
She claimed her white

A Sin Beneath the Cosmos

A tale the cosmos told
Would wrench and gut your soul.
Under the celestial blanket,
A shadow walked alone.

His mind, once sane,
Had turned to wicked bane.
Quandary of forgive and forget
Was shattered after this act.

Violet sky whispered to him,
A lullaby of deadly sins.
It spoke of vengeance cold and grim,
For the vice she did to him.

Purple and blue, he left her frame
In the field of lavender seeds.
Her corpse reeked of flowers sweet
As he hummed the lullaby, lost in defeat.

Home on the Hill

Across the mustard field
Far on the hill
When the saffron blaze,
With rays so soft,
Shined into my home.
Made my walls yellow
And my princesses mellow.
My goddess of love
Soaked the honey glow.
The melody of her laughter
Blessed my soul.

The Price of Green

They played with toys
I played with coins
They threw tantrum
I sat alone
Why do they get the dream I hold?

Their cool summer
I longed madly
They had pity
I had envy
Yet we had a bond indeed

They begged to be free
I carried it at fifteen
They poisoned for fun
I slogged endlessly
Why was my world so green?

They stayed in shirts
I changed to coats
They stayed the same
I outgrew my green
After all, growth came at the cost of envy

The Rebellion

A bureau that claimed
Peace and gains,
Kept the streets clean
With fear and chains.

Two decades of republic,
Citizens failed.
The straw did finally break
When a color was banned.

A rebellion, so silent,
Graffiti on walls, whitewashed.
Magenta ink permeated.
Scrubbed, yet it stained to stay.

Whispers in air,
Their hands in hand,
Would shake the Bureau's reign.
History shall remember their name!

Alas! The history bent,
Cuffs on their hands
Hushed the whispers,
Erased them without a trace.

The Softest Strength

Nella's skin was peachy.
She bruised her heart easily.
Her father dismissed her quality,
her principle and honesty.
Her mother's words were stormy,
mistook her warmth, saw it weakly.
Her neighbors laughed hysterically,
as she stood up to the bully.
Everyone wished to reshape her entirely,
to turn her warmth to fury.
Nella sobbed bitterly,
but stood her ground firmly.
Her patience was rooted deeply,
her peach-sweet whisper disarmed the bully
Melted his icy guard completely.
All those who mocked watched shamefully,
swallowed their words, once thrown so freely.
Her affection wrapped all cozily,
made them question their cruelty.

Intuition's Last Cry

Turn around,
turn around.
This sky seems fake.
This road is a bait.

Stop now,
stop now.
These lights are dim,
danger lurks unseen.

Hear me out,
hear me out.
I'm sure it's footsteps
ask your shadow, it'll tell!

Hide away,
hide away.
This indigo night
is lengthening your way.

Run fast,
run fast!
It's got a knife!
Don't turn, too late!

I warned you,
I warned you.
Now nobody to help,
they'll find you in a bag someday.

Trickstress

Every full moon
she drops by.
Nothing shines
but her princess coat
and her silver beret
over her bun so low.

Common or diplomat,
child or man
you fear the Vixen,
the arched brow,
the silver tongue,
if guilt stains your hand.

The charm in her voice,
the confidence in her lie.
She'll snap your twisted sin
with her own bent ethics.
She'll strip you down
with words unforeseen.

There's room to wriggle,
an offer to make.
Could be your house

or just a date.
Are you willing?
Your choice to make.

How does she know?
All ask, worried.
Is she a witch,
or the devil in disguise?
They cry or beg
for whatever's at stake.

Little do they know,
she tricks her way.
Everybody has a lie
tucked away.
She merely hints,
and they give it away.

Blush Beyond Takes

Behind the camera
Under the dew,
Daisy and Cornell
Worked with a crew.

Cornell ran with scripts and boards,
Daisy fixed the actors' suits,
But all saw their improvised role.
Beyond the sets, glances stole.

His eyes were fixed,
Yearned her deep.
In her salmon shirt,
She enchanted him.

All day long,
On weary toes,
Bites were shared,
Hands were held.

Daisy's pink cheeks
Blushed repeatedly.
Cornell's heart
Skipped a beat.

At the dawn,
Their lips met,
Making the horizon
Flush rosily.

The Urban Ecstasy

City that's always in sight,
Billboards with dental smiles.
Stars unnoticed under lights,
As urban ecstasy climbs.

Blue, pink, green, yellow,
What a neon glow!
Sugary, salty, yummy bites
Taste buddies danced in delight.

Fluorescent synthetic garments,
For every range of skin.
Body positivity heavily guarded,
Life is good on the fiftieth floor.

Sink beneath the neon shine,
See the cracked roads.
Those smiles in the billboards
Sob tears of coal.

The rats of party dystopia
Rule the burdened land.
Water as good as sewer,
Obesity and diabetes flare.

Chin up before you drop below,
Keep your eyes on the neon glow.
Does it not make you happy?
The perfect colourful show.

The Obsidian Key

My family has an obsidian key,
Sharp-edged, uneasy, and hidden from me.
They said my hands were too small
To hold the secrets it hid.

The key was to a door unclean,
Guarded by shadows that screamed.
My folks carried a legacy,
One I had yet to claim.

My mother pacified me,
Said, *"Stains are part of every tree.*
Every family has a key,
Buried in their roots, deep."

Melted snow and falling leaves,
My frame grew tough,
And beard on cheeks.
Mind still terrorized by the reeking door.

Mold wrapped around the bricks,
My uncle silenced the wailing things,
Passed the key with its rusty ring,
And waited for the door to creak.

Darkness awaited, so pitch.
The torch barely lit the path within.
Chained to the bars
Was a tortured being.

It leaked juices I couldn't relish,
And flesh too tough to eat.
I couldn't digress,
I opened the door to a cannibalistic feast.

Now my heart pumps blackened ink,
I am the heir to devour the weak.
Every family has a key—
One that holds their legacy.

Colourless Bride

They assumed I mourned
His passing, indoors.
Was a strong soul,
Smiling through pain.

I still heard his voice
*"Do not cry,
You'll be alright."*
How could I ignore?

He never ate for taste.
Salt and sugar were a waste.
He consumed my love from grains.
I acquired bland for taste.

He'd say, tracing my beige drape,
"It brings a shine to your gaze."
Norms of Neverland,
Deaf to his ears.

Their condolences failed,
Couldn't embrace
The warmth of a beige drape,
The comfort of curd and rice.

Ladies from upstairs
pity the colourless bride.
How do I tell them
the dull sparks my life?

The Maroon Day

It's not fresh nor dry,
Just the right amount of stale.
The clots in his dream
Change to maroon as day breaks.
Passion restrained for wage.

He'll build the foundation
His elders failed to lay.
He won't see any light,
They won't allow him into dark,
Stuck forever in the maroon day.

Blazing Quills

The great Prince of Velmoria
Wrote beneath the ancient tree.
His spark of thought
Saved the falling inns
Words—shattered glass
Could ignite a crimson war,
But nothing could stop the boy,
Whether to please or destroy.

Penniless pockets,
Yet he could not forfeit
His endless writing treats.
He walked the earth,
Swam the seas,
Climbed the mountains,
And fell from trees
All for stories that speak.

He troubled the queen,
He cursed the king,
For each siege declared
On quills and verses.
His fingers, inked with red,
Smeared on threads.

And yet, no chains and commands
Could sever the fire that enraged

Minty Sole

Skipping down the street,
steps light as breeze.
Minty eyes and whimsical smile,
Sees radiance in everything.

Lilly's spirit so lively
Sipped on herbal brew.
Her refreshing tone
Reflects her gentle soul.

Suitcase yet to unpack,
A home yet to make.
This city is exciting,
vibrant, and soothing.

She sells fresh cookies,
that melt you all the way.
Uncle John and Aunty Lia
Blush with that sweet taste.

Nothing to hide, no one to lie,
Her heart always rests light,
Floating through life, embracing!
In her minty sole.

www.ingramcontent.com/pod-product-compliance
Lightning Source LLC
Chambersburg PA
CBHW071313130726
47997CB00007B/2529